A COMPLIMENTARY COPY from—

GARRARD PUBLISHING COMPANY
1607 NORTH MARKET STREET
CHAMPAIGN, ILLINOIS

DISCOVERY BOOKS

Reading Level: Grade 3
Interest Level: Grades 2–5

Net $1.98, postage paid

The Discovery Books are prepared under the educational supervision of

Mary C. Austin, Ed.D.
Reading Specialist and
Professor of Education
Western Reserve University

A DISCOVERY BOOK

by Lynn Groh

illustrated by Ted Lewin

GARRARD PUBLISHING COMPANY
CHAMPAIGN, ILLINOIS

P. T. Barnum

King of the Circus

Especially for Susan

Manufactured in the United States of America

Library of Congress Catalog Number: 66-10070

Contents

P. T. Barnum: King of the Circus

CHAPTER

Chapter 1

A Week in New York

So this was New York!

Young Taylor Barnum slushed through the snow on Broadway. Mr. Brown, his neighbor from Connecticut, rode a horse. Together they drove a herd of cattle down the street to the market.

It was a cold January day in 1822. Taylor's mop of curly brown hair was hidden under a stocking cap. His big brown eyes were bright with excitement.

This was the biggest day in all his eleven years. Most boys from Bethel, Connecticut, only dreamed of going to New York City. He was there! Taylor could not keep his eyes off the rows of shops and brownstone houses. Some of them were three and even four stories high.

At Fulton Street the cattle were put in pens behind the market buildings. Mr. Brown took Taylor to an inn.

"You will have a week to see the sights while I sell all my cattle," Mr. Brown said.

Proudly the boy signed his full name in the guest book: Phineas Taylor Barnum.

"That is a lot of name for a young lad," the landlord said.

"I was named for my grandfather, Phineas Taylor," the boy explained. "Folks in Bethel call me Taylor."

"Well, Taylor, I hope you enjoy your week in New York."

"Oh, I certainly will!" Taylor said.

He went out to the sidewalk. Which way should he go first? The shops had no show windows. Some had signs, such as "Clothing" and "Umbrellas and Parasols." Others had the names of the owners. Some had no signs at all.

If he had a store, Taylor thought, he would put up signs so people would know what was inside.

A street peddler passed, chanting his wares. Taylor followed him a short way. His eye caught a sign, "Billiards." He pushed open the door.

Several men stood at a table. They were playing a game. "Go away! No children allowed," a man shouted.

No children were allowed at the Park Theater, either. There seemed to be no place where children could go. Taylor watched the busy street. People rode by in carriages and sleighs. A horse trolley stopped at the corner. Several people got off and hurried away. Everyone had some place to go.

Taylor saw a mother and two children enter a building. "Museum," the sign read. Taylor went in too.

The museum was dusty and had a bad smell. But Taylor's eyes grew big when he saw a giant cobra in a glass cage. He looked closer. It was only a stuffed skin.

There were other stuffed snakes, birds and animals. In one room were wax statues of George Washington and other famous people. Best of all was a real, live orangutan from Borneo.

"I wish there had been an elephant," Taylor said to Mr. Brown that night. "I would certainly like to see an elephant."

"There have been only two elephants in America. Both are dead now," Mr. Brown said. "You will have to settle for the orangutan."

The next day Taylor saw a sign that read "Confectionery." That meant cakes, candies and other goodies. Taylor went in. The store also had toys such as he had never seen before. He stared at the shelves around him.

Taylor had only one dollar to spend. He chose carefully. He bought a gun which shot a stick across the room, a top, a knife, and a tin watch. Then he picked out a breastpin for his mother.

Suddenly he saw a glass jar filled with molasses candy. Taylor wanted some but he had no money left.

"Will you take back the knife and give me some candy in its place?" he asked the shop lady.

"Yes, I'll make a trade with you," the lady said.

Taylor ate the candy. He just had to have some more! He traded his watch for more candy. Before the day ended he had traded all his toys for candy and had eaten all of the candy. He had nothing to take home!

The week ended. Mr. Brown rented a one-horse sleigh and they bundled into it. Taylor's pockets were empty. But his head was full of marvelous stories to tell about his week in New York.

Chapter 2

A Boy on His Own

Taylor stood behind the counter of his father's new store. A pencil was tucked over his ear. He was fourteen now, and he tried to act grown-up.

His father was waiting on a customer.

"So you have given up farming," the customer said.

"Yes," Mr. Barnum replied sadly. "I couldn't get any work out of Taylor on the farm. Maybe he will do better in the store."

Taylor knew that he would do better. "I like head work," he said. "Farming is only hand work. Besides, it's lonely."

It was not lonely in the store. Farmers came to buy hoes and plows. Their wives brought in butter, eggs and bundles of goose feathers to trade for household goods.

Peddlers came in wagons from New York and Boston. They traded their wares for the butter, eggs and feathers. In those days, money was very scarce. Business was done by trading. Taylor liked to trade. He became good at it.

In winter there was hardly any outside work to do. Men sat around the stove in the store. Grandfather Taylor often joined them. He loved to tell jokes and riddles.

"Why is a dog's tail like an old man?" he would ask.

"Because it is on its last legs," was the answer.

The men talked about strange creatures which might live in faraway lands. In those days people knew little about the rest of the world. Often sea captains made up stories about seeing mermaids, giants and tribes of two-headed people. Some people believed these stories.

Taylor was not so sure. But he thought the world would be more exciting if there were mermaids and giants. He often kept the store open late at night so the men would stay and entertain him with their storytelling and jokes.

Suddenly his happy life ended. His father died. Mr. Barnum had many debts. When these were paid the family had no money left. The store was sold.

Mrs. Barnum and the four younger children went to live with Grandfather Taylor. But Taylor got a job. Although he was only fifteen he had to help support the family.

He worked in a store in a small village a mile from Bethel. It was very dull there and Taylor did not earn much money.

"I'll never get ahead here," Taylor told his grandfather. "I would have a better chance in a big city."

"Then go!" Grandfather Taylor said. "You will never get anywhere unless you really try."

Taylor found a job in a Brooklyn store, across the river from New York. No matter how long and how hard he worked, he was paid the same wage.

"I should work for myself," Taylor said. "Then I could make good trades and keep the money."

"Come back to Bethel," Grandfather Taylor said. "I will let you have my carriage house for a store."

Taylor put shelves and a counter in the carriage house. He brought supplies from New York. He painted signs to advertise his wares. Still he was not ready to open the store.

"Well, what are you waiting for?" Grandfather Taylor asked.

"For the crowds!" Taylor said. "I'll open on Military Training Day."

ALE
OPENING
MILITARY
TRAINING
DAY

In those days, all men had to train as soldiers. On Military Training Day they put on a show. They marched and drilled to band music.

Farm people came to town, their wagons loaded with things to sell or trade. It was like a county fair.

Taylor's store was on the main street. The big sign he had painted and put over the door caught everyone's eye: "P. T. Barnum, Fruit and Confections." Smaller signs listed his wares.

Mothers came in and bought fruit and candy fresh from New York. They bought toys for their children. There were pocketbooks and jackknives for the boys. For the girls there were combs, beads and rings. There was a barrel of ale for the thirsty soldiers.

"You earned more today than you spent on your store!" Grandfather Taylor said that night.

"And everyone for miles around knows that P. T. Barnum has a store in Bethel," Taylor said. "It pays to advertise!"

Chapter 3

In Search of a Trade

Taylor's business grew. His love for a shy young girl named Charity Hallett also grew. Soon they were married. Together Taylor and Charity worked and saved. Finally they were able to build a big new store. They lived in two floors above it.

"Some day we'll live in a castle," Taylor boasted.

The store was successful, but Taylor was restless. He looked for more exciting things to do. He bought a printing press and published a weekly newspaper.

Then he started a lottery. Lotteries were very popular in Connecticut. The people had little entertainment. They liked the excitement of buying a chance on a big prize. Taylor liked the fun of riding all over the state to sell tickets.

Charity looked after the store and cared for their little baby, Caroline. "Taylor likes to be among people," Charity told friends. "He is happiest when he is in a crowd."

Men still gathered in Taylor's store to talk. One day a friend told Taylor, "I saw a strange sight over in Litchfield.

There was a dog with two tails. One of the tails was three feet long!"

"Really! If I had that dog I'd show it around the country," Taylor said. "Is it for sale?"

"I'm sure you could buy it. It wouldn't cost more than five or ten dollars," the friend said.

Taylor ran to saddle his horse. As he started to ride away the friend called, "I forgot to tell you that the dog was coming out of a leather-tanning factory. One of the tails was a cow's tail that he was carrying in his mouth!"

The other men laughed loudly. Taylor was angry for a moment. Then he laughed too. He had learned to take a joke from Grandfather Taylor.

Once again Taylor's good life ended.

The government passed a law forbidding lotteries. Many people owed Taylor for tickets they had bought. Others owed him for groceries they had bought. No one could pay him. Taylor had to sell his store.

"We will go to New York to seek our fortune!" he said to Charity.

For seven months Taylor worked at different jobs in New York. He was a clerk in a store. He sold caps on the street. He wrote for the newspapers. None of these jobs seemed to be right for Taylor.

Then one day he heard of a strange woman named Joice Heth. Joice claimed to be 161 years old! She said she had been George Washington's nurse when he was a child.

GEORGE WASHINGTONS NURSE
161 YEARS!

Taylor became Joice Heth's manager. He took the old woman from town to town. He put advertisements in the newspapers. Crowds came to hear Joice Heth sing hymns and quote from the Bible. She told many stories about George Washington's childhood.

Many people believed Joice Heth. "See how old and feeble she is? She must be 161!"

Others argued, "No one lives 161 years. Joice Heth is a fake and P. T. Barnum is a humbug!"

Barnum only said, "She *could* be 161, and anyway she puts on a good show!"

Soon Barnum tired of Joice Heth. He hired a manager for her. Then he became manager of a road show. The actors went by wagon through many states. They were away from New York for many months at a time.

Charity was left alone with Caroline and her new baby, Helen. Once when Taylor returned home, he found all of his family sick. There was no one to take care of them.

"There will be no more traveling for me," Taylor promised Charity. "I will stay in New York and take care of my family. I will find something to do."

But Taylor had learned one thing from his adventures. Show business was the trade for him!

Chapter 4

Barnum's American Museum

Taylor was reading the want ads in the newspaper. "Oh, Scudder's American Museum is for sale!" he cried.

"That dusty old place!" Charity said. "I'm not surprised that the owners want to get rid of it."

"I would like to own it," Taylor said. "I could make it the biggest show in town."

Taylor went to talk to his friend Horace Greeley, editor of the New York *Tribune*.

"*You* buy the American Museum!" Horace said. "What will you use for money?"

"Brass, for of silver and gold I have none!" Taylor laughed.

He went to the office of the museum owner, Mr. Olmsted.

"You want to buy the museum, but you have no money!" Mr. Olmsted said.

"But I will have money," Taylor argued. "I will buy the museum on credit. Each month I will make a payment on it."

Mr. Olmsted did not think much of the plan. But Taylor had always been a good trader.

"If I fail to pay even one month, you can take back the museum and keep all the money already paid," he said. He knew he would pay on time.

Mr. Olmsted finally agreed. He also owned a billiard parlor next door to the museum. "You must rent that too, so I will be sure of getting some money out of you," he told Taylor.

"I can't rent the parlor and a house too," Taylor said. "We will live in the billiard parlor."

The billiard parlor was one long, narrow room. It was dark and gloomy. Charity used heavy curtains to divide it into rooms. She made it as cheerful as possible. Taylor was very proud of his museum. Charity wanted to do anything she could to help him keep it.

The museum was a fine, five-story gray stone building. It was on one of the busiest corners in New York, at Ann Street and Broadway. The rooms were large with high ceilings. Sweeping staircases led to the upper floors.

Taylor had no money to buy new exhibits, but he made the old ones look like new. He hired an artist and promised to pay him later. The artist painted jungle scenes on the walls of the lobby. He painted jungle settings for the stuffed birds, snakes and animals.

Charity washed the clothes of George Washington and other wax statues. She helped wash the glass exhibit cases.

On opening day the museum looked like a gay carnival. New Yorkers had never seen anything like it.

The artist had painted pictures, one story high, on the outside of the building. Flags and pennants flew from the roof. A huge sign spelled out "Barnum's American Museum."

A brass band played from the first floor balcony. The music could be heard for blocks around.

Taylor had used his old trick of opening on a holiday. It was New Year's Day, 1842. Crowds filled the streets. The people heard the music and hurried to see what it was all about.

Taylor wandered among the people, listening. "This is Scudder's old museum, but who is Barnum?" they asked.

Barnum smiled to himself. It would not be long before all New York would know who P. T. Barnum was.

Chapter 5

"It Pays to Advertise"

Six months passed. One day Mr. Olmsted stopped at the museum to collect a payment. He could hardly believe his eyes. The museum had never been like this!

People moved from room to room, laughing and calling to each other. Some crowded around a stage where a dog was working a big spinning wheel.

EGRESS
WAY
FLEAS
ALIVE

Another room had a huge sign on top of a glass case: "THE INDUSTRIOUS FLEAS!" Inside the case, fleas pulled tiny carts much bigger than themselves. Nearby, the Mechanical Man played chess with a customer.

There were posters everywhere! They were painted in bright colors, with many capital letters and exclamation points.

Arrows pointed to rooms where one could see other fabulous sights. There was a giant Arab, whom Barnum called "The Tallest Man in the World." There was a Bearded Lady, a woman with long flowing whiskers like a man. And there was a Living Skeleton, a man so skinny one could almost see his bones.

Strange music by the African Marimba Band floated down the stairs. Mothers sat with their children eating picnic lunches. They had come to spend the day in Barnum's American Museum.

Mr. Olmsted found Taylor in his office, munching sandwiches from a paper bag.

"Is this the way you always eat your lunch?" he asked.

"I will eat sandwiches every day of the year until I have paid you for the museum," Taylor said.

"With these crowds you should own the museum by the end of the year," Mr. Olmsted said.

"It costs a lot of money to bring the crowds in," Taylor said. "I have to give them something new all the time. I want everyone in town to be talking about the museum."

Taylor used advertising to keep people talking. He announced each new exhibit with big ads in the newspapers. He passed out handbills on the streets. There were always giant, flashy posters.

Sometimes the posters were more interesting than the exhibits. For his Fejee (Fiji) Mermaid, ads showed a beautiful woman who was part fish. The "mermaid" in the museum was an ugly, twisted creature. It was really the upper body of a monkey joined to the tail of a fish.

His newspaper friend, Horace Greeley, scolded Taylor about his ads.

"Your poster for Niagara Falls is a full story high," he said. "But your model of the falls is only eighteen inches tall!"

HALF
FISH
NIAGARA FALLS
THIS WAY
FEJEE
MERMAID

Taylor grinned mischievously. "But it really does have water!" he laughed. "The poster is only to catch the eye and bring the people in. Once they are inside, I give them a good show for their money."

"But what about that mermaid?" Greeley asked. "People must know it is a fake. There is no such thing as a mermaid!"

"When I was a barefoot boy back in Connecticut, I believed there were mermaids, because I wanted to believe it," Taylor said. "People like to think there *could* be mermaids and other wondrous things. It makes life more exciting."

"Maybe we are all boys at heart," Greeley said.

Chapter 6

General Tom Thumb

The Barnum family sat in their living room watching a five-year-old boy sing and dance.

He looked like a normal boy in every way but one. He was only 25 inches high!

"He's no bigger than your thumb," Charity said.

"Then we will call him Tom Thumb, like the little fellow in the fairy tale," Taylor said. "For an extra joke, we will call him a general!"

"General Tom Thumb" was really named Charles Stratton. He was a midget. Soon he would become the most famous midget the world has ever known.

Tom Thumb and his parents moved into the billiard parlor with the Barnums. Taylor wanted no one to see the midget until he appeared on stage at the museum. Secretly, he taught Tom Thumb songs, dances and other acts. In two weeks they were ready.

Barnum's famous posters were put up. His handbills were given out all over the city. He bought full-page ads in the newspapers. These all advertised General Tom Thumb as "The Twenty-Five-Inch Man!" and "The Smallest Person That Ever Walked Alone!"

Tom Thumb did more than walk alone. He danced and told funny stories. He imitated Napoleon, Cupid and Greek gods. Dressed as a soldier, he marched up and down singing "Yankee Doodle."

"The midget is one of Barnum's freaks," people said. "But at least he is not ugly."

Tom Thumb was as lovable as any child. Besides, he was very talented. Soon he was the talk of New York. The museum would not hold the crowds that came to see him.

Barnum's Museum made so much money from Tom Thumb that Taylor paid all of his debts. He hired a manager to take the midget on a tour of the United States.

Taylor stayed in New York. Now he had a small fortune. He used it to collect animals from all over the world. As a boy he had wanted to see an elephant. Now he owned ten elephants! He had the first giraffe and the first hippopotamus ever seen in the United States. He brought lions and tigers from Africa. These were all exhibited in the museum. P. T. Barnum had the first zoo in the United States!

"You are my good luck charm," Taylor told Tom Thumb. "We have won America. Now we will conquer Europe!"

Taylor and Tom sailed to England. Queen Victoria had heard of the famous midget. She asked Taylor to bring Tom Thumb to the palace.

"This is a step up in the world for the barefoot boy from Connecticut!" Taylor said.

When the English heard that Tom Thumb had entertained the queen, everyone wanted to see him. Princes and nobles paid large sums to have him act in their castles. Crowds went to the theater to see his public shows.

Later, Taylor and Tom Thumb toured France, Belgium and Holland. Kings and peasants alike cheered the "Twenty-Five-Inch Man."

It was three years before Taylor and Tom Thumb returned to the United States. P. T. Barnum was now famous all over the world. He was called "The Great Showman."

He was also a millionaire.

Chapter 7

The Swedish Nightingale

Taylor Barnum had built his castle at last. It was an Oriental mansion in Bridgeport, Connecticut, like one he had seen in England.

Taylor and Charity stood in the great hall, welcoming guests to their house-warming party.

A thousand people came. They were rich and poor, famous and unknown. P. T. Barnum was a friend to everyone.

"What did you say you named this house?" a friend asked.

"Iranistan," Barnum answered. "I'm going to retire and stay here with my family."

"You can afford to retire!" called a heckler in the crowd. "You must have made a lot of money from your freaks and phony mermaids!"

"I always gave the people a good show," Barnum replied. His voice was jolly, but the cutting remarks hurt his feelings.

Barnum rented his museum to a Mr. Greenwood. Barnum became mayor of Bridgeport. Then he started building a model town of his own. He called his town East Bridgeport. He spent a lot of time playing with his three daughters.

But Barnum could not stay away from New York. Two or three times a week he went to the museum and mingled with the happy crowds. People who recognized him called, "There's P. T. Barnum!" The children gathered around to ask questions about his wild animals. Barnum's greatest joy was that he was known as "The Children's Friend."

One day Barnum visited Horace Greeley. "I can't stop thinking about a better show," Barnum said.

"You built the greatest show in the country," Horace said. "What more can you do?"

"I'm tired of being known for freaks and stuffed monkey skins. I'm going to bring Jenny Lind to America," Barnum said.

"Jenny Lind? Who is she?" Horace asked.

"The Swedish Nightingale," Barnum replied. "She is the most famous singer in Europe."

"But Americans have never heard of her," Horace argued. "You will lose your fortune! Americans like carnivals, not opera singers."

"I will show you," Barnum said stubbornly. "I will show America I am more than a 'carnival man.' "

Barnum's posters and advertisements soon had everyone talking about the Swedish Nightingale. Many people were angry. "What does Barnum know about fine music?" they said. "No doubt he will put Jenny Lind in a box and show her off like one of his freaks."

Still, when Jenny Lind finally did appear, no one wanted to miss the show. Barnum rented a famous hall, Castle Garden. The first concert was held there. Every seat was filled and many people stood.

Barnum stood in the wings when Jenny Lind went on stage. He watched the faces in the audience. What would people think of the "carnival man" now?

At first there was a murmur of disappointment. They expected a great singer to be beautiful. Jenny Lind was very plain. But when she began to sing, a change came over her.

"Her face glowed, and she looked like an angel," one writer said later in his review. All the critics warmly praised her beautiful voice.

Happily, Barnum set off on a tour of the United States with his famous singer. They traveled for nine months. Jenny Lind gave nearly a hundred concerts. Crowds followed wherever she went. Women copied the dresses and hats that she wore. Parents named their baby girls for Jenny Lind. Little girls played with Jenny Lind dolls. "Jenny Lind" became one of the most famous names in America.

Barnum made a lot of money from the Swedish Nightingale's concerts. But money meant little to him now. The really important thing was that now people said, "P. T. Barnum is truly the Greatest Showman on Earth. He cannot fail at anything!"

Chapter 8

Beginning Again

Barnum and Tom Thumb were ready to sail to Europe again. This time there were no cheering crowds to see them off.

Barnum had lost his fortune. He had loaned thousands of dollars to a man who manufactured clocks. The man did not use the money honestly. He had to close the clock factory. Barnum was left with many debts to pay.

People who had been friends would not speak to Barnum now. They said he was being punished for his tricks.

Others were very kind. Tom Thumb had his own traveling show. He rushed to help Barnum.

"Maybe people will still like us in Europe," Barnum said.

More than ten years had passed since their first tour. But Europeans had not forgotten P. T. Barnum and General Tom Thumb. Their shows drew bigger crowds than before. Once again the two friends made a fortune.

Barnum used all his earnings to pay his debts. He returned to New York penniless.

"Now I will start from the beginning again," he told Horace Greeley. "I am

taking over Barnum's American Museum."

Barnum worked hard to find wondrous exhibits. He brought a Sacred White Elephant from India. From Africa came a midget elephant he called Tom Thumb.

Then he built the first American aquarium, in the museum's basement.

He filled it with man-eating sharks, white whales, and strange tropical fish.

There were exhibits from America too. Barnum brought the West to New York. Indians performed war dances. Grizzly bears and sea lions did tricks. Barnum added buffalo, wolves, and mountain lions.

But Barnum's bad luck had not ended. One night his museum burned to the ground. Most of his animals and exhibits were destroyed. Barnum was heartbroken, but he built another museum at once. Two years later, his new museum burned too!

"Maybe this is a sign that you should retire," said Horace Greeley. "You are the Father of American Show Business. You deserve a rest now."

"And besides, I am 60 years old and a grandfather!" Barnum laughed. "It's time for me to make room for younger men."

But the old showman could not stay retired. In his old age, P. T. Barnum was to plan the greatest show the world has ever seen.

Chapter 9

The Greatest Show on Earth

Ten thousand people crowded into a huge tent in Brooklyn. All eyes were on a big arena in the center of the tent.

Taylor stood watching the people. He wanted to see how they would look when the show began.

There was a fanfare of trumpets. A brass band struck up a lively march. The Grand Parade began and the circus was on!

There had been circuses before, but never one like this. Barnum had collected every circus act he could find. He put them together in one great show. He added dazzling costumes for actors and animals. Then he thought up The Grand Parade. The actors rode around the arena in golden chariots.

The circus was a big hit. Everyone

called it “The Greatest Show on Earth.”

Restless Barnum was not satisfied. As always, he dreamed of a bigger and better show. He kept looking for new acts for his circus.

“There must be a limit to how many acts you can have,” a friend said.

“If there is a limit I have never reached it,” Barnum replied.

He went to Europe to search for the most daring acrobats, and the most unusual animals. In Italy he found a goat that rode a horse bareback. In France he found "The Human Projectile." A woman was shot from a cannon into the air, and then caught by a man on a flying trapeze.

When he reached Germany, Barnum received sad news. Charity had died. Taylor sat alone in his hotel room. He did not feel like looking for circus acts. Soon he returned to America.

In times of trouble, Barnum always worked harder. Now he took his circus on a tour of the country. Actors and animals traveled in wagons and carriages. These were painted in bright colors and plastered with colorful circus posters.

The "circus train" was a strange sight, winding down the lonely dirt roads that crossed America.

Then another circus appeared, called International Allied Shows. It had just returned from a tour of South America. The circus was not as large as Barnum's, but it drew big crowds.

Barnum met with the manager of the other circus, James Anthony Bailey. "If we fight each other we will both lose money," Barnum said. "Why don't we *join* each other?"

"The show would be too big," Mr. Bailey said. "It would take all night to show all of our acts!"

"Then we will show several acts at a time," Barnum said. "Each act will have its own ring."

19
PTB

Bailey agreed. And so the three-ring circus was born.

The new partners planned their grand opening for March 18, 1881, at Madison Square Garden in New York. Barnum had his famous posters ready: "P. T. Barnum's New and Only Greatest Show on Earth!"

Saturday night before the opening, the partners held a circus parade on Broadway. Dozens of men carried torches. One hundred golden chariots, carriages and circus wagons rolled down the street. Some of them were pulled by trained zebras and deer.

There were 338 prancing horses and 20 elephants. Hundreds of circus actors, in glittering costumes, marched to the music of four loud brass bands. One of

EATEST
SHOW
EARTH

the bands was made up of Indians. The parade was three miles long!

It seemed that everyone in New York lined the streets or leaned from windows. The people cheered until they were hoarse. Then an open carriage came by. There sat P. T. Barnum himself!

"The King!" the people shouted.

The King of Show Business stood and lifted his hat. The crowd could only see the broad smile on his cheerful face. They could not see the tears in his eyes.

Taylor was remembering an eleven-year-old boy who had once walked down Broadway, driving a herd of cattle.

Fifty-nine years had passed. Now all New York cheered P. T. Barnum, the man who had everything the boy had dreamed of.

Chapter 10

The Last Act

"Our agent thinks he can buy Jumbo!" Barnum excitedly told his new wife, Nancy. She was a young English girl whom he married after Charity died.

"You mean the giant elephant in the London zoo?" Nancy asked. "I've seen him many times."

"I even rode on his back once," Barnum laughed. "He is the biggest elephant ever captured."

Barnum wired his London agent to offer $10,000 for Jumbo. To everyone's surprise, the zoo officials accepted the offer. They said Jumbo was so old he would have to retire soon anyway.

Barnum was delighted. But when the English heard that Jumbo had been sold there was a great uproar. Children wept. People wrote angry letters to the newspapers, the zoo officials, and even to Barnum.

Jumbo had been in the zoo for seventeen years. He was everybody's pet. People felt he belonged in England. Finally Queen Victoria commanded the zoo to return Barnum's money and to keep Jumbo.

Barnum did not want his money. He wanted Jumbo. There was a court trial.

The judge ruled that Jumbo belonged to Barnum.

Jumbo quickly became the pet of Americans too. He traveled with Barnum's circus for three and a half years. Over a million children rode on his back. Jumbo was so famous that his name became a word in the dictionary, meaning "very large."

Barnum himself was very old now. But he had not thought of retiring. He was nearly 80 when he decided to take his circus to England. Nancy went too.

He did not know how the English would receive him. They were still angry at him for taking Jumbo. But all hard feelings were put aside when

The Greatest Show on Earth opened in London.

Barnum himself appeared most nights at the arena. Between acts, he rode around the ring in a shiny black carriage. Everyone stood and saluted the grand old man who had brought joy to so many people.

When he returned to America, Barnum became ill. Soon it was clear that he could not live much longer. He lay in bed receiving many visitors. He had something cheerful to say to each one.

"I wish I could see what the newspapers will say about me when I am gone," Barnum told Nancy.

A reporter heard of Barnum's wish. A few days later the New York *Evening Sun* printed his obituary so he could read it before he died. The story of his life, with pictures, almost filled one page.

P. T. Barnum looked at the big, bold headline at the top of the page. A happy smile crossed his face. The headline read:

"THE GREAT AND ONLY BARNUM"